W9-CDK-124

Dogs

Dalmatians

by Jody Sullivan Rake

Consulting Editor: Gail Saunders-Smith, PhD

Consultant: Jennifer Zablotny, DVM
Member, American Veterinary Medical Association

Capstone
press
Mankato, Minnesota

Pebble Books are published by Capstone Press,
151 Good Counsel Drive, P.O. Box 669, Mankato, Minnesota 56002.
www.capstonepress.com

1 2 3 4 5 6   11 10 09 08 07 06

Library of Congress Cataloging-in-Publication Data
Rake, Jody Sullivan.
  Dalmatians / by Jody Sullivan Rake.
  p. cm—(Pebble Books. Dogs)
  Summary: "Simple text and photographs present an introduction to the
dalmatian breed, its growth from puppy to adult, and pet care information"—
Provided by publisher.
  Includes bibliographical references and index.
  ISBN-13: 978-0-7368-5333-0 (hardcover)
  ISBN-10: 0-7368-5333-2 (hardcover)
  1. Dalmatian dog. I. Title. II. Series.
SF429.D3R35 2006
636.72—dc22   2005023969

Note to Parents and Teachers

The Dogs set supports national science standards related to life science. This book describes and illustrates dalmatians. The images support early readers in understanding the text. The repetition of words and phrases helps early readers learn new words. This book also introduces early readers to subject-specific vocabulary words, which are defined in the Glossary section. Early readers may need assistance to read some words and to use the Table of Contents, Glossary, Read More, Internet Sites, and Index sections of the book.

Table of Contents

4

Firehouse Dogs

Dalmatians used to help firefighters. Today, dalmatians are mascots for fire stations.

Dalmatians are
family pets.
They like to be
with their owners.

From Puppy to Adult

Dalmatian puppies are white at birth.
Their spots begin to show in three weeks.

A female dalmatian
may have as many as 15
puppies in one litter.

Adult dalmatians have
short white fur
with dark spots.
Their floppy ears often
have so many spots
that they look black.

Dalmatian Care

Dalmatians have light skin.
They can get a sunburn.
Owners must be careful
not to keep them
in the sun too long.

Dalmatians like
to live indoors.
They do not like
to live in doghouses.

Some dalmatians
are born deaf.
Owners can train them
to learn hand signals.

Dalmatians need food,
water, and exercise
every day.
They need love
and attention too.

Glossary

deaf—unable to hear

litter—a group of young born to one female at the same time

mascot—an animal that represents a team or group

signal—a sign used to tell an animal or person to do something

sunburn—burning and redness of the skin caused by staying in the sun too long

train—to teach an animal to obey

Read More

Allen, Jean. *Dalmatians.* Dog Breeds. North Mankato, Minn.: Smart Apple Media, 2003.

Stone, Lynn M. *Dalmatians.* Eye to Eye With Dogs. Vero Beach, Fla.: Rourke Publishing, 2005.

Internet Sites

FactHound offers a safe, fun way to find Internet sites related to this book. All of the sites on FactHound have been researched by our staff.

Here's how:

1. Visit *www.facthound.com*

2. Type in this special code **0736853332** for age-appropriate sites. Or enter a search word related to this book for a more general search.

3. Click on the **Fetch It** button.

FactHound will fetch the best sites for you!

Index

Word Count: 133
Grade: 1
Early-Intervention Level: 12

Editorial Credits

Martha E. H. Rustad, editor; Juliette Peters, designer; Jo Miller, photo researcher; Scott Thoms, photo editor

Photo Credits

Capstone Press/Karon Dubke, 14; Cheryl A. Ertelt, 6; Corbis/Kalish/DiMaggio, 4; Getty Images Inc./Photonica/Gone Wild Limited, 16; Lynn M. Stone, 12, 18; Mark Raycroft, cover, 1; Norvia Behling, 20; SuperStock Inc., 10; UNICORN Stock Photos/ Gary L. Johnson, 8